FORGOTTEN

Loving Those
We've Left
Behind

FORGOTTEN

Loving Those
We've Left
Behind

Tom Ervin

The Holy Bible, English Standard Version® (ESV®)
Copyright © 2001 by Crossway,
a publishing ministry of Good News Publishers.
All rights reserved.
ESV Text Edition: 2016

Archway Publishing books may be ordered
through booksellers or by contacting:

Archway Publishing
1663 Liberty Drive
Bloomington, IN 47403
www.archwaypublishing.com
1 (888) 242-5904

ISBN: 978-1-4808-5911-1 (sc)
ISBN: 978-1-4808-5912-8 (e)

Library of Congress Control Number: 2018901897

Print information available on the last page.

Archway Publishing rev. date: 02/15/2018

Contents

To Nancy

Thanks for all your love, patience, and
support these fifty-three years!

Nancy

Before we begin, I want to introduce my wife, Nancy. After fifty-three years of marriage, I have learned about the countless ways she has enriched my life and, frankly, the lives of everyone she meets. Because she is mentioned in this book and has contributed to its content, I want you to meet her.

It happened on the day after Thanksgiving in 1962, when I was twenty-two and she was twenty-one. I was a senior at the University of Detroit, majoring in marketing, and she was a junior at Marygrove College, a women's college, majoring in economics. We had both, unknowingly, been invited by our respective professors to attend a career day being offered by the owner of Hudson's Department Store for those seeking business careers.

About forty students from various colleges in the Detroit area were gathered in the store's auditorium for a presentation on the merits of a career at Hudson's. After the presentation, we were taken on a tour of the store and its many departments. It was then that I saw her walking about twenty feet ahead of me. She was wearing a bright red dress and heels. On the front of her dress was a series of little heart-shaped black buttons. She was tall and had an attractive way of walking. To top it off, she had a beautiful face, with blue eyes and a little chin that dipped downward. At first glance, she was a knockout! I couldn't take my eyes off her throughout the tour, which lasted about a half hour. Later, she told me that she had spotted me also and wanted to attract me, even though she'd thought I needed a haircut. Well, she didn't just attract me. She owned me!

After the tour, we had lunch in the cafeteria. When I looked for her, I was happy to see she had a seat available next to her. We talked all through lunch, and I learned where she went school and where she lived. Her name was Nancy, and her dad was the police chief in a neighboring suburb not far from my house. I know you won't believe this, but after lunch, we both went our separate ways without my getting her last name and phone number. Two days later, I had the bright idea that I would call her dad's police station and ask for her last name and phone number! When the police dispatcher answered my call, I explained that I had just met Nancy and wanted to take her out on a date but needed her last name and phone number. She replied, "Oh, that's our Nancy!" She then proceeded to give me the missing information. (You and I know that couldn't happen today.) When I called her and told her I was Tom Ervin, who met her at Hudson's, she said, "Yes, I remember!"

We were married twenty months later, after I had enlisted in the Navy reserves and she had graduated. As the years went by, our family grew to six children. Nancy gave birth to four boys, and we adopted two girls. We also brought nine other children into our home, each of whom stayed with us up to a year until being adopted through various adoption agencies. As you will see later on in this book, we also became quite involved with children in Detroit's inner city. Everything we did, we did together.

We started eight different businesses, including a very successful publishing business that Nancy created and managed for many years. That company paid for the private high school tuition and college degrees of all our children. They had no student loans, except for one of our daughters who took out a loan to finance her law degree after receiving her bachelor degree at the University of Michigan. Two of Nancy's greatest attributes are kindness and courage. Her favorite saying is, "Keep on marching!"

My Premise

The wildflowers on the cover of this book will never become part of a wedding bouquet. Nor shall they be selected from the local flower shop for a friend recuperating from an illness. You won't see them on the tables at a retirement party upon the successful conclusion of a fifty-year career.

These flowers grow on a hillside beneath Mt. Rainier in the state of Washington. These red, yellow, pink, and white beauties take to seed every spring, grow, bloom, and perish completely unnoticed by humanity. They are among the millions of forgotten flowers that grow all over the world in quiet solitude.

Each summer, Nancy and I drive up north from the Detroit area to a small town on the eastern shore of Lake Michigan. Charlevoix is a typical tourist town that swells in the summer and empties out when the cold north winds begin their annual trek south from Canada. We drive Interstate 75 most of the way. The passing scenery is breathtakingly beautiful, especially the deep pine forests that abound on both sides of the highway. If you look closely, you'll see that the ground is saturated with wildflowers of various colors and sizes. Taken together as a huge mosaic, they refresh the soul and are a vital contribution to the good of the earth. I'm only able to see them as we speed along the highway at seventy miles per hour because I'm looking for them. Most travelers, anxious to reach their destinations, probably don't see them even for a brief glance.

Actually, those wildflowers' unnoticed existence is much like the unnoticed existences of people we know or don't know who may live nearby.

As Thoreau once wrote, most people live lives of quiet desperation whose primary objective is to somehow make it through each hour of each day. And their desperation usually goes unnoticed by many of us, as we command resources that help us live lives of relative satisfaction.

Who are the forgotten ones in your life? Could they be those members of your own family who are physically close but not emotionally as close as they should be? Have the relationships, once very loving, become somewhat frayed, or are they on the verge of collapse?

And how about those people who live in our communities, whose plights are ignored by those of us who could help? Will we consider reaching out to strangers who don't have the resources to help themselves?

It is my belief that each of us must answer these questions for ourselves. Of course, the great irony of our lives is that whatever we take is only temporary, because we can't take anything with us in the end. Speaking of the end of our lives, how will we finally judge the allocation of our time spent here? I do believe in the saying, "To whom much has been given, much will be expected."

If the wildflowers below Mt. Rainier are typical, they will bloom without recognition. This may also be true of many people living right now in your family, neighborhood, or community. Will these people be like the unseen flowers deep in the forest? Or will they be loved?

Why Is the Discussion of Love Important?

Love exists everywhere in nature and is not unique to humans. All animal species do two things essential for preservation of their species: reproduce and raise offspring. Parental animals often sacrifice themselves to protect their babies. They do this instinctually, but another word for it is *love*. Likewise, affectionate courting is widely seen in nature. There is no doubt that love is a critical factor for our survival.

A Daughter's Story

I recently attended a man's retirement party. One of his daughters was the first to speak. She approached the microphone and said it was hard for her to speak about someone she loved so much. She went on to say that her dad loved her with such an intense and unconditional love all her life that she grew up believing she could face any challenge and be successful. Upon graduating from college, she enlisted in the Marine Corps and rose to the rank of captain. She was sent to Iraq while the Iraq War was raging. She was responsible for the lives of hundreds of fellow marines while there and served her country with distinction. Just as the flowers in the forest need seeds to grow, she needed what we all need to grow, love.

How about the timing for this discussion about love? Have you ever seen families and communities in such discord?

We definitely have a world of haves and have nots when it comes to love. Some are born into loving situations and complete the remainder of their lives safely within the cocoon of love. Others have never been loved and really don't know what love looks or feels like.

I think you would agree that there is too little love in the world. Hatred, anger, and self-centeredness seem to contribute to the crumbling of human relationships on every level. Yet, each of us has an enormous capacity to love. As Dr. Martin Luther King Jr. said, "I have decided to stick with love. Hate is too great a burden to bear." Can't each of us be a better person than the person we each are today?

Those words really resonate with my way of looking at myself. We should never be completely satisfied with who and what we are. There is so much potential in all of us to do so many good things. The greatest among these things is to lift up someone who is hurting.

Just so you know where I'm coming from, I have been loved every day of my life. Yes, I am one of those few people who has always known I was loved. I am the oldest of five boys and a girl born to our parents, who remained married for sixty-two years, until our father's death at age eighty-nine in 2002. I married the love of my life. Yet I am keenly aware of those who prod through their daily journeys either still searching for love or having abandoned the search entirely.

Under various circumstances, as mentioned previously, nine non-biological children came and went from our house over the years in addition to our own kids. At one time, we had eight teenagers living under our roof. It's amazing that the roof didn't blow off the house with all of that excitement.

Nancy and I have spent many years working with various families and individuals living in Detroit's inner city. We have seen children abandoned, families on the brink, hunger, despair, and widespread hopelessness. It is my intent in this book to use other people's true stories as well as my own experiences and observations after seventy-six years of life. My objective is to recommend ways to help make your time on earth one of always growing in love and joy. I break the topic of love into two categories.

Loving People We Know

We begin with how we feel about ourselves. Then we move into romantic love, which is what we often think of when the word *love* arises. In this form, passion, desire, and yearning for the loved one can be overwhelming. We want to be with our loved ones and to receive love in return. Our loved ones' responses to us have a huge effect on our sense of self-worth. Rejection can traumatize us physically, mentally, and emotionally. Conversely, a mutually shared love with another, a love that is sustainable over a long period, allows us to bring the best of ourselves to each day. This section concludes by looking at love of other family members.

Loving People We Don't Know

This love for other people emanates from many different motives. Among them are a sense of fairness, a sense of justice, empathy, compassion, identification with a person or group, or just the desire to help someone improve upon his or her present situation and quality of life. Most people love family members and friends. Loving someone we don't know is a different thing entirely, but it is so necessary if we are to leave a world wherein our children and grandchildren can live in peace.

We will explore these two kinds of love in their various forms, including examples of each and suggestions on how they can be best expressed.

1

Loving People We Know

Loving Yourself

Are you a forgotten flower? Buddha is quoted as saying, "You can search throughout the entire universe for someone who is more deserving of your love and affection than you are yourself, and that person is not to be found anywhere. You yourself, as much as anybody in the entire universe deserves your love and affection."

Let's talk about you. Do you love yourself? God only made one of you, so God must think you are very special. If you think highly of yourself or possess an adequate sense of self-esteem, you will be able to use more of the many gifts you have and enjoy a more fulfilling life than if you suffer from low self-esteem. Your childhood continues to have a major impact on how you feel about yourself throughout your life. If your parent or parents encouraged you, recognized your achievements, and loved you with unconditional love, you have learned that you are lovable.

Self-esteem or the lack thereof is the primary indicator of whether you will choose a path that permits you to enjoy all you can be or that robs you of the fulfilling life you would have otherwise realized. Unfortunately, many of us are subject to the influence of negative people whom we allow to impact our vision of ourselves. These negative influencers can come in many forms: parents, spouses, siblings, other family members, social media "friends," classmates, employers, co-workers, teachers, and many others.

How to Improve Your Self-Esteem

If you have low self-esteem, there are things you can do to feel better about yourself:

- Take care of your personal appearance: Good personal hygiene, regular grooming, and the right clothing can be big boosts to your self-esteem. How you look and feel is everything! Take the time and effort to look good. It will go a long way toward improving your self-pride.
- Be a good person: It's hard to feel good about yourself if you know your life is on the wrong track. You are the sole guardian of your self-esteem. People who strive to do good things feel good about themselves. They live their lives with fewer regrets. A life, however, that is filled with regrets is tough to live with every day. You can control how you

perceive yourself simply by doing the right thing in your decision-making.

- Forgive yourself: We all make mistakes. No one is perfect. When you make a bad decision or do the wrong thing, learn from your mistake so you don't repeat it. Then forgive yourself and move on.

- Be kind to others: Others will treat you in direct response to how you treat them. Your sense of self-esteem can improve by following the golden rule: "Do unto others as you would want done unto you." Being kind to others yields two terrific benefits to you: You know you are doing the right thing, and you'll feel better about yourself when receiving others' kindness in return.

- Don't compare yourself to others: Comparing yourself to others is a complete waste of time. There will always be someone smarter, richer, more popular, etc. Who cares? Be grateful for your life, and celebrate the success of others.

- Volunteer: Consider joining a volunteer organization. Mahatma Gandhi believed, "The best way to find yourself is to lose yourself in the service of others." What are your hobbies or interests? Join a local volunteer organization that works in an area you feel strongly about. Let's say, as an example, you love pets. You could join an animal rescue organization. You would be doing something you believe in while meeting other people who share your passion. The friendships you develop could also greatly improve how you feel about yourself. Studies have also shown that the biggest benefit of volunteerism is the increase in self-esteem felt by volunteers because they are making a positive difference in the world.

The Evil of Egomania

While we're talking about self-esteem, we would be remiss if we didn't also discuss those who are over the top with their self-esteem, commonly referred to as egomaniacs. Most dictionaries define egomaniacs as people who are obsessively absorbed with themselves.

The behavior of an egomaniac is almost always destructive to the person himself or herself and to everyone around. My dad often reminded me of his favorite Latin proverb, "*In medio stat virtus*." The English dictionary translation is, "Virtue stands in the middle." Dad interpreted the proverb as, "In the middle stands the truth." So self-esteem, similar to many other human qualities, shouldn't be too low nor too high.

Romantic Love

Is your spouse a forgotten flower? Bob Marley once said,

> "You may not be her first, her last, or her only. She loved before. She may love again. But if she loves you now, what else matters? She's not perfect—you aren't either, and the two of you may never be perfect together but if she can make you laugh, cause you

to think twice, and admit to being human and making mistakes, hold onto her and give her the most you can. She may not be thinking about you every second of the day, but she will give you a part of her that she knows you can break—her heart. So don't hurt her, don't change her, don't analyze and don't expect more than she can give. Smile when she makes you happy, let her know when she makes you mad, and miss her when she's not there."

I have strong feelings about romantic love. We only live once. When two people decide to devote their one and only lives to each other, it is a really big deal! I think the traditional wedding vows contain so much wisdom. Let's examine each vow:

To Have and to Hold

These words say a lot about the couple's commitment to each other. It implies that each party has tremendous trust in the other—so much so that this vow's implied promise is that each will give over his or her emotional, mental, and physical wellbeing into the care of the other. Also implied is that the couple will participate in the most intimate human relationship possible, the act of lovemaking.

From This Day Forward

Henry Miller said, "The one thing we can never get enough of is love. And the one thing we never give enough is love." With such an immense decision to trust one's wellbeing to another comes responsibilities. The biggest and most essential responsibility is loyalty to one's partner so that the couple avoids acts of betrayal. When someone cheats in a marriage, the cheater damages both himself or herself and the cheated-upon partner. Trust must be the cornerstone of a good relationship. Without it, chaos ensues unabated! Think of the damage done to a partner who is cheated upon. His or her self-esteem and faith in people takes a terrible blow, one from which total recovery is impossible. No one is capable of hurting another more than someone who was trusted and violated that trust. If you are incapable of being loyal to your partner, don't get married. All you're going to do is hurt someone who doesn't deserve to be hurt.

For Better, For Worse

Friedrich Nietzsche said, "It is not a lack of love, but a lack of friendship that makes unhappy marriages." A lifelong commitment can't be conditioned upon a carefree life. Nobody gets through this life without challenges, some trivial and some life changing. Whatever life delivers to your door, the two of you must face it together.

Because you and your partner are unique individuals, you will not always react to adversity in the same manner. You have to allow for the other person to react in whatever manner is most comfortable, even though it may not be the way you would react. Sometimes one partner is vocal while the other partner is quiet and doesn't want to talk about it. Every good marriage is built by both people making an effort to understand the habits of the other and making attempts to accommodate the differences.

For Richer, For Poorer

One of the more damaging impacts on a marriage is a financial crisis. Many marriages have floundered and failed because of the pressure exerted by too many financial obligations and not enough money to meet them. Arguments and accusations can become everyday events when the need for enough money seems to be out of reach. Married partners may have completely contrary approaches to the subject of finances. One may be a saver and the other a spender. In many cases, outside financial counseling may be the only way both partners can come together on a plan that will hopefully put them on a strong financial footing. The plan could be to cut costs, bring in more income, or a combination of both. Whatever the eventual solution, both parties will probably have to compromise on previous untenable positions and meet somewhere in the middle.

As strange as it sounds, there could be too much money. One of the partners may enjoy the security of adequate financial strength and like to live conservatively without a need to impress people. The other partner, however, may need to compensate for low self-esteem by using money to elevate how others perceive him or her.

In Sickness and in Health

If both partners were healthy at the time of the union, the ensuing sickness of one of the partners can be traumatic. It can become especially troublesome if the ill partner was the biggest or sole breadwinner. If one partner has been diagnosed with a long-term illness, there must be a healthy dialogue between the two partners as to a plausible course of action.

Nancy and I attended a wedding many years ago. At the reception, the father of the bride rose to offer a toast to the newlyweds. He said, "Marriage is like a carriage being pulled by two horses. Both horses, being of equal strength, pull their share of the burden. If one horse becomes weary or ill or unable to keep up the pace, the other horse must pull harder so that the carriage can safely reach its destination." Marriage is a partnership. Both partners must be flexible enough to respond adequately to whatever needs to be done in unforeseen circumstances.

Until Death Do Us Part

Marriage is a lifelong promise, not to be entered into if there is not a genuine intent to honor that promise. In the year 2007, a most poignant story about Supreme Court Justice Sandra Day O'Connor appeared in the news. Her husband of many years was in the latter stages of Alzheimer's disease. She would come to visit him regularly at the nursing home where he resided. On one of her visits, he announced to her with great joy that he had fallen in love with a lady who was a fellow patient. During her subsequent visitations, husband John, age seventy-seven, and his new love would spend time together holding hands. She knew, of course, that the disease had seriously hampered his cognitive abilities. As Justice O'Connor would relate to the press after John's death, although it was an upsetting experience for her, she loved her husband and wanted him to be happy in his final days. This is a dramatic example of living out the true meaning of "until death do us part."

It is not uncommon in our society, however, to see husbands discard their aging wives in favor of younger women. This is the most hurtful and ultimate betrayal. After a woman has given her youthful body to the procreation of a man's children and endured all the physical, mental, and emotional difficulties involved in child bearing and childrearing, she is cast aside like yesterday's newspaper. All her efforts devoted to building a family in an atmosphere of total trust and all the compromises she has made to allow the marriage to flourish are forgotten. Another insult is the fact that when the young couple was married, they probably had a modest income and limited financial resources. With his wife's help, the man struggled through the lean years and now is more appealing to a younger woman because he has money. This injustice is often committed to satisfy one of the great evils of the world, the male ego.

How to Keep the Romance Alive

There are a few steps both partners can take to keep the romance alive and well.

Be Honest

Knowing that the most necessary ingredient in a happy marriage is trust, you can't nurture a trustful long-term relationship without honesty. It would seem obvious that honesty is important, but in too many instances, political correctness has become a terrible substitute for honesty. If you have children, they will learn from your behavior whether to be honest or not.

Be Respectful

It doesn't matter whether one partner is more intelligent than the other. You owe your partner and your partner's opinion respect. If you don't show respect for him or her, you are, in effect, telling other people they don't have to respect your spouse either. Isn't a lifelong commitment of marriage deserving of as much happiness as possible as a reward? If the answer is yes, it is your responsibility to build your partner's sense of self-esteem up rather than running it down. I will always remember a dinner we had with another couple. In the midst of our conversation, the other man said that he had a college degree while his fiancée only had a high school diploma. She was quite embarrassed, and we felt uncomfortable. I guess he thought his remark was supposed to show that he was superior to her. The opposite was true. His remark was hurtful and callous.

Say "I Love You"

It doesn't matter how long you are married, your spouse must hear the magic words on a regular basis. You and your spouse are two very different people. Yes, you have some common attributes, but each of you will react to events with dissimilar behaviors. This is why you often don't really know how your partner is feeling. You might think that things are going well and that the other person doesn't need to be reminded that you love him or her. Sometimes you should say "I love you" when you are feeling warmhearted. Other times, you should say it because your partner is dealing with a difficult issue, and hearing the magic words might be just the right positive reinforcement he or she needs to move forward. Never say those words if you can't say them with sincerity. Those are not words you use when you are just going through the motions. False sincerity will create a worse reaction than if you had said nothing.

Be a Listener

The world doesn't revolve around you anymore! There are now two lives with the same commitment but different points of view. All unions include two unique individuals. As the old saying goes, "Opposites attract." The best partnerships are created when both people are good, attentive listeners. All too often we hear the lament, "You don't listen to me."

Share the Load

In earlier times, most marriages had clearly defined responsibilities for each partner. That is not true today. Many more women work outside the home than ever before. This reality calls for a new approach to all the chores required to move a marriage and/or family forward. Hopefully, the partners discuss their time constraints and mutually devise a plan that meets their common objectives. Every couple approaches the topic of sharing the load in its own style. This is fine as long as both partners come to an agreement on the best way to proceed.

Leave Old Arguments Behind

When a couple is engaged in a disagreement, one of the partners, in order to win, may bring up something in the past. Never do that! Stick to the current facts, and don't burden your partner by creating guilt for some previous misstep. Repeated reminders of past problems will drain the life out of an otherwise healthy relationship.

Be Kind

Do you treat a complete stranger with more kindness than your spouse? It is actually quite common, so unfair, and over time, very detrimental. It is my fervent hope that at the end of my life, my spouse will feel that I caused much more kindness than unkindness in our marriage.

Respect Privacy

There are certain situations in your marriage that, out of respect for your partner and the marriage, must remain private. It is never appropriate to discuss your intimate marital situations or your partner's faults and shortcomings with someone else. You are to be your partner's cheerleader and always speak well of him or her.

Respond to Your Warmhearted Impulses

Respond to your warmhearted impulses. There are hopefully times in your marriage when you feel a strong surge of emotional affection for your spouse. You should act on that feeling by at least saying, "I love you!" Better yet, bestow some affection on him or her that truly expresses how you are feeling. A spontaneous act of affection is a beautiful thing!

When the Kids Come Along

Another common pitfall arises when children come along. Until the birth of the first child, it is just the two of you. Each partner receives the undivided attention of the other. When the first and possibly subsequent children join the family, however, I have seen a spouse give much more attention and affection to the children instead of the other spouse. This is not a good development for the future of the marriage. I understand the obvious attraction of a small, innocent child, but the marriage must always come first. If Mom and Dad love each other, the kids will be happy.

Good Manners

Even though both partners enter into an intimate relationship, good manners and the extension of common courtesies are important. There are times when a spouse must respect the other's need for privacy. Many of the polite gestures performed during courtship should not end at the altar.

Say "I'm Sorry!"

People don't apologize anymore. Have our egos become so fragile that we can no longer admit that we said or did the wrong thing that upset or hurt another person? We must be able to reach down and offer a sincere apology when the situation demands it. If we are parents, we have a particularly strong obligation to apologize to our children; we must teach them that apologies can be the only appropriate action in some circumstances. Otherwise, they will behave as too many people do today: blame someone else for their transgression.

Be Forgiving

As apologies are important, so is forgiveness. God forgives us throughout our lives. Can't we do the same with our loved ones? Forgiveness can be verbal or nonverbal. With all the stresses we face in our modern times, we don't need to also bear the burden of a grudge against our partners. Move on while facing forward, not backward! Life is too short not to forgive and forget. Remember, you're not perfect either.

Engage in Surprising Acts of Kindness

Don't just do something nice for your spouse on the "supposed to" holidays, such as Valentine's Day and Sweetest Day. These days are motivated by guilt and a sense of obligation. Be creative and surprise him or her when it is least expected. That's when it really makes a strong and often lasting impression.

I will never forget a huge surprising act of kindness Nancy prepared for me when I returned home from work on a Friday evening after a harrowing week at the office. When I came through the door, she had all six kids sitting in the living room and announced that she had called my boss earlier in the week to see if he would let me take the following week off from work. She had our bags packed and in the car, and we were going to walk out the door and drive to Metropolitan airport, where we would stay the night in a nearby hotel and then fly first thing the next morning for a one-week stay at a beachside resort in Nassau, Bahamas. She had reserved the airport hotel and the hotel in Nassau and arranged for my in-laws to stay with the kids. That was a surprising act of kindness I shall never forget. That's love!

Obviously, your surprising act of kindness does not need to be as dramatic or as costly as a surprise trip to the Bahamas. It could be flowers on just an ordinary day. When asked why you brought them on a non-holiday, you could reply that you love your spouse every day, not just on holidays. You've got to be creative to keep the romance glowing.

Go Out on a Date

Many marriages can become stale because both partners get
into a rut. Even though the partners are burdened with the
responsibilities of earning a living and managing a home,
you still must make time for just the two of you as you did
during your courtship. Plan to go out on a date. It could
be out for dinner or dinner and a movie. It is important
that the two of you have a chance to talk away from other
distractions, and it is great for the relationship that you have
fun together. This is an example of "marriage insurance."

Unconditional Love

Are you able to love unconditionally? Unconditional love is
love at its very essence. Pure and unaffected by circumstance,
it stands alone as the most perfect kind of love we could ever
attain. Because our spouses, like ourselves, are imperfect and
capable of errors in judgment from time to time, can we
look beyond present infractions toward a lifetime of loving
them? Even though your lover is not perfect and never will
be, you can still strive to create as perfect a love as possible.

You may often be embarrassed by your loved one's behavior.
In these instances, unconditional love is only possible if you
are capable of forgiveness. And forgiveness is only possible
if you are committed to a spousal relationship built on
unconditional love. You may respond by saying that this
kind of love is really difficult. Look back on your life thus
far. Every truly worthwhile accomplishment of your life

has been difficult. So why should the goal of achieving unconditional love be any less difficult?

When You Are Attracted to another Person

You may become attracted to someone you meet along life's journey. This new attraction may be more powerful than the attraction you presently have or ever had with your spouse. So, what do you do?

I would like to offer a suggestion. You have to live with yourself twenty-four/seven. What kind of "yourself" do you want to live with? Will you compromise your value system in exchange for some short-term gratification? Would you stray from your commitments to your spouse because your ego has been stroked by the attention of someone else? If so, you'll end up being someone whose commitment is not reliable and can no longer be trusted. As you peel away your value system, you are left with someone you don't recognize? While this self-destruction is underway, what price will your spouse and perhaps children have to pay in terms of emotional and mental suffering? If you are looking for a happy life with your partner, stay loyal and keep life simple. Life is hard enough without complicating it with poor life-changing choices that only breed guilt and lifelong regret.

Loving Family Members

Is your family member a forgotten flower? Mother Teresa once said, "We think sometimes that poverty is only being hungry, naked and homeless. The poverty of being unwanted, unloved and uncared for is the greatest poverty. We must start in our own homes to remedy this kind of poverty." Mother Teresa is telling us that love should flourish in our own homes. Do you have a family member who needs your love and attention? We have a small plaque in our house that says, "Bloom where you're planted." As I said earlier, you may have teenagers who are hard to love because they are in that rebellious stage we all go through. Their days are filled with emotional turmoil brought on sometimes by insurmountable peer pressure or possible bullying. In such environments, many teenagers don't like themselves. This is all the more reason that you must be their soft pillow when they come home.

Your Teenage Children

Our own teenage years were tumultuous; we had a lot to deal with. There were raging hormones, peer pressure, self-doubt, puberty, and relations with the opposite sex, to name a few. Today, with the advent of social media, we should add cyberbullying to the list. Millions of our teenagers suffer from vicious, very public attacks on their self-esteem, leading them to retreat into drug use or, even worse, suicide.

They really don't like themselves very much, and they love to take it out on you, their parents. They will often act out in ways that target you in order to vent their anger and frustration. The reason teenagers attack their parents is that they know deep down that you are there to stay, that you will not abandon them. They know from a lifetime of experience that you are their rock and that even when they are disrespectful or cruel to you, you will not leave them. As much as their behavior is distasteful and actually unappreciative of your parental efforts throughout their lifetime, you've got to love them through it.

Your Adult Children

This is advice for those of you whose adult children marry. In order to support their marriages, you must practice unconditional love for their spouses. Your child's spouse may or may not be the person you would have selected. If the latter is true, you must forever keep those feelings to yourself. Your job is to support the union and never allow your behavior to cause a breakup that might have otherwise been prevented. You don't need that burden going forward. You must make the decision to love whomever your child loves!

The same principle applies to your new in-laws. In order to promote as much harmony as possible for the newly married couple, you must embrace the new in-laws and whatever baggage they might bring along.

The truth is that once a parent, you are a parent forever. Your adult children still need you, even though they may not admit it. There is nothing magical about your child reaching the age of adulthood. Your job is not over when your children turn twenty-one. They still have problems as adults that may require your involvement. As adults, however, their problems are usually more serious than those encountered during childhood.

Your Parents

Do you continue to return love and affection to your parent(s) as you grow older and more independent? Or do you fault them for the mistakes they may have made that negatively affected your childhood? Regardless of their performance as your parent(s), you must decide how you will treat them the rest of their lives. Will you take the high ground and love them or cast them out of your life?

I believe in living a life with the fewest regrets possible. Fewer regrets means less baggage to carry around the rest of your life. Take the high ground by keeping your parent(s) a part of your life. It'll make it easier for you to live with yourself.

Your Siblings

How about your brothers and sisters? Unlike parents, who usually exercise rather predictable behavior, you and your siblings undergo many changes on the journey to adulthood. Each of you will have different experiences that will affect your opinions and reactions. This is especially true if one of you experiences a traumatic event; trauma can rapidly reshape our perceptions. Also, siblings' friendships outside the family can alter their behavior and future familial interactions.

Of course, the most impactful change in siblings' lives is when they choose their partners, if they do. Each partner will exercise great influence and can either enhance or disrupt your sibling relationships. If you see disturbing signs that the previous closeness you once shared is unraveling, you must make a choice. Will you try to accommodate the change in order to maintain family unity, or will you allow the family to fracture? Things change, and people change. Maintaining family unity is also tested when your parents are no longer here to be the glue that holds everyone together. You may have to become that glue!

2

⁓⤳⁓   ⁓⤳⁓

Loving People We Don't Know

Jesus says in Matthew 5:46, "For if you love those who love you, what reward do you have? Do not even the tax collectors do the same?" (All bible quotes are from the English Standard Version).

Now we turn to the more difficult and unnatural form of love: loving people we don't know. (I must admit that your situation may ironically be that dealing with strangers is easier for you than working with family members.)

It is my firm belief, formed over many years, that loving family and friends is not enough. In order to leave a better, safer world for our children and grandchildren, we need to improve the lives of the suffering multitudes one person at a time.

Loving people we don't know is not always based upon feelings. It is based upon our personal value systems. Some of these values that could motivate us to love others might include a sense of justice, a sense of fairness, and a sense of compassion.

The Story of Alan Turing

The following true story about Alan Turing spotlights the issues of justice, fairness, and compassion. Alan Turing (1912–1954) was an English computer scientist and mathematician. He was a leader in the development of theoretical computing. He designed the Turing machine, which can be considered a model of a general purpose computer.

In 1936, Turing published a paper that is now recognized as the foundation of computer science. Turing analyzed what it meant for a human to follow a definite method or procedure to perform a task. For this purpose, he invented the idea of a "universal machine" that could decode and perform any set of instructions. Ten years later he would turn this revolutionary idea into a practical plan for an electronic computer, capable of running any program.

After two years at Princeton, developing ideas about secret ciphers, Turing returned to Britain and joined the government's code-breaking department.

In July 1939, the Polish Cipher Bureau passed on crucial information about the Enigma machine, which was used by the Germans to encipher all its military and naval signals. After September 1939, joined by other mathematicians at Bletchley Park, Turing rapidly developed a new machine (the "Bombe") capable of breaking German Enigma messages on an industrial scale. It is believed his work in deciphering the Enigma machine shortened World War II by two years, thus saving an estimated 14 million lives.

A few years after the end of the war, the British government became aware that Mr. Turing was gay. At the time, the British legal system considered it a crime to be a gay person. It offered Turing the two alternatives of either two years in prison or the voluntary use of a drug designed to sterilize him. In 1954, he died eating an apple laced with cyanide poisoning at the age of forty-one.

No other person in human history is said to have saved 14 million lives. Yet, Alan Turing unnecessarily suffered terribly in the last few years of his shortened existence.

I've told this story as a dramatic testimony to the unfairness that often dominates so many people's lives. When I was young, I would see unfairness and ask, "Why doesn't God do something about this?"

Now that I'm much older, I've come to the conclusion that it's my responsibility to do something. It's also your responsibility to do something. It does no good to just complain about the state of our world. For those of us who have talents and resources to create a world of greater fairness, we must act. That is why we are here.

Forgotten Flowers on Detroit Streets

Reverend Faith Fowler's Story

This story is about Reverend Faith Fowler, pastor of Cass United Methodist Church located in the inner city of Detroit, Michigan. The following episode happened in 1993.

People came knocking on Reverend Fowler's church door all hours of the day and night. They made demands reasonable and unreasonable. One night in December, six months after she became pastor, there was another of those persistent knocks at the door. When she partially opened the door to see her visitor, it was a prostitute who worked the corner where the church was located. She was angry and very animated while telling Reverend Fowler, "You've got to do something about her." It was only upon fully opening the door that Fowler could see a twelve-year-old girl standing beside her. The woman said the girl was also working her corner as a prostitute and that she didn't want her to "end up like me." When Fowler looked into the little girl's eyes, she realized her purpose wasn't her life and the frustrations that go with being an inner-city pastor. It was the people who needed help, such as this twelve-year-old girl. As she recalled many years later, "People's lives were at stake. They were paying a heavy physical and emotional price." At that moment, she realized, "I had to get over myself." She decided to dedicate herself to establishing an organization that could reach out to those in need.

Now, twenty-three years later, she continues to direct the efforts of Cass Community Social Services in addition to her role as pastor. This organization, with her leadership, has helped thousands of men, women, and children who have been homeless, addicted, and mentally ill, HIV positive, and abused find love and acceptance.

Reverend Fowler is a very accomplished person with a healthy sense of self-esteem. She has, however, taken an additional step forward that many of us have not considered or may not want to consider. She has made a lifelong decision to put the abandoned, homeless, and addicted people in our society ahead of her own personal priorities. As she stood at her church door that night, she made a deliberate and life-changing decision to balance her love of self with the love of others. More importantly, she executed this decision consistently for twenty-three unbroken years of effort for the benefit of complete strangers.

How about you and me? Will we decide to better balance our love of self with our love of others? As the song says, "What the world needs now is love, sweet love." I think most of us would agree that many human relationships are quite frayed and in need of nurturing. There are many factors causing deterioration in relationships. One of the more obvious causes is the widespread retreat into social media as a poor substitute for person-to-person interactions. The ability to reach out and love those in need is always within each of us.

Forgotten Flowers on the Battlefield

Malik Abdul Hakim's Story

I want you to read the following true story that appeared in *The New York Times* in 2015. In all my seventy-six years of living, the following story has moved me like none other! It was the front-page story and was about a sixty-six-year-old farmer living outside Kabul in Afghanistan. Mr. Hakim was a member of the Afghan Red Crescent, which is dedicated to protecting human life and health and is part of the International Red Cross Movement.

Photo Credit: Bryan Denton/*the New York Times*/*Redux*
Malik Abdul Hakim, who returns bodies of Afghan forces and insurgents to their loved ones, in Kandahar, Afghanistan.

In 2008, Mr. Hakim was contacted one day by a high member of the Taliban, which was at war with the central government headquartered in Kabul. The Taliban wanted him to go to the government authorities and request the return of the body of a senior Taliban official who had been recently slain in a battle with government forces. They wanted his remains reunited with his family for a proper burial. He agreed to go to Kabul to see if he could persuade government officials to release the body.

The government official became upset with Mr. Hakim and asked why he wanted a Taliban body released while the bodies of slain government soldiers were not being released by the Taliban. Mr. Hakim called the Taliban and told them the government would not release the body until the Taliban agreed to return the body of a slain government soldier.

Thus began the most profound demonstration of love for people Mr. Hakim did not know. As of the 2015 publishing date in *The New York Times*, he had delivered 713 bodies of Taliban and government soldiers back to their families. In 2014 alone, he delivered 313 bodies. In a battle that took place near his home, he found the bodies of twenty-eight Taliban fighters, all of whom he returned to their families. Despite the viciousness of Afghans killing fellow Afghans, Mr. Hakim, as you can imagine, is loved by many people on both sides of the war.

If the body is unidentifiable, he takes a photo and buries the deceased in a plot of ground on his farm that he has designated as a cemetery. He has a simple index card attached to each photo showing the location and date of the battle where the person was slain. Some relatives have traveled to his farm and retrieved loved ones with the help of his photos and filing system.

Mr. Hakim had two sons and a son-in-law. His son-in-law was an employee of the government who drove a water truck used to spray dirt roads to keep down the dust. One Sunday, his two sons decided to ride along with him while he drove on his assigned route. None of the three young men returned home that night. Mr. Hakim later learned that the Taliban had killed all three because they were driving a government truck. Despite his terrible personal loss, he continues to return the bodies of both Taliban fighters and government soldiers.

When asked why he continues to perform these incredible acts of kindness, he replies, "I do it for God and for the powerless."

Comment

How could Mr. Hakim work day after day in the heat of Afghanistan to do the unthinkable? In his words, he did it for the love of God and for the powerless. We know he was a member of the Red Crescent, which is a sister organization to the Red Cross. So, as a Red Crescent member, he was obviously inclined to come to the aid of strangers. He was well known in his area and was sought out by the Taliban because it was aware of his compassionate nature. This story would never have made international prominence, however, if it had only been about the delivery of one body. No, his love of God and humanity has driven him to continue on his own year after year. He loves God enough to serve strangers by returning the remains of their family members.

I believe the most compelling fact of Mr. Hakim's mission is that he has continued to return Taliban bodies to their families even after the deaths of his two sons and son-in-law, all of whom were killed in cold blood by the Taliban. It would seem his love has no limits.

I realize this is probably one of the most extreme examples of reaching out to offer a helping hand to strangers while expecting nothing in return. It's obvious, however, that he goes to sleep each night safe in the knowledge that he brought love to the powerless. If he can love that much, what are the limits of our love?

Forgotten Flowers in Inner-City Schools

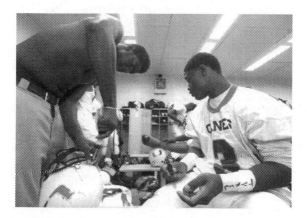

Detroit News, September 24, 2009 Detroit Douglass High School varsity quarterback Vic Davidson adjusts his helmet so it'll fit junior varsity running back Ronald Gordon. The players are forced to share equipment because of a lack of funds in the program. (David Guralnick/*Detroit News*)

Most of us live in urban areas where some people live below the poverty level. Not unrelatedly, much is written and reported about the lives of young black males in our modern society. Most of these stories are about crime and violence they perpetrate. I would like to offer a first-person eyewitness account of some of these young men's lives and daily circumstances. I really don't think many people understand how precarious and traumatic some of their lives are. Come along with me, and look behind the headlines.

Our journey into Detroit's inner city began with the front-page article shown above. I happened to see it in the Sunday edition of *The Detroit News*. At the time the article appeared, we had two grandsons playing high school football at their respective schools in the northern suburbs. Their suburban athletic programs had everything needed to field a well-equipped team. I was appalled that the inner-city Detroit high school boys didn't have enough helmets for every player. Some players had to wait on the sidelines until a player came off the field to get the equipment they needed. They also had no physical trainers or medical staff at their practices and only an ambulance service at games. Many didn't have cleats, or they had old cleats that were not their size.

Nancy and I met with an official of the Detroit Public Schools Community District to learn more. Finally, we decided to concentrate on one high school (Henry Ford) nearest our home. The head coach of the varsity football team invited us to work with him and his assistants in order to help create a better athletic experience for his players. During the three years I spent there, Henry Ford had an enrollment of fourteen hundred students. Every student was of African American descent. In the entire Detroit high school football league, every team player was African American with the exception of Southwestern High School, which also had Mexican American students. It is from my daily interactions with them on and off the football field that I have compiled memories of many incidents in these players' lives.

At the age of sixty-nine, I walked into a whole new world. I didn't know anything about these teenage boys and their lives, and they certainly didn't know what to make of me. The head coach was also the math teacher in the school. He was a young African American man who was married, with two sons and a daughter. His wife was also a teacher in Detroit. While in college, he converted to Islam and is a very loyal practitioner of his faith.

After spending every day with this coach during the long football season's practices and games, I realized he is one of the finest people I have ever met. No matter how upset he might become during a practice or game, he always treats each and every player with respect. If you have ever watched head coaches and their behavior during the ups and downs of a game, I think you'll agree that a coach who treats every player with respect in all chaotic game situations is a special person. Happily, we were successful! In 2011, our second year together, we finished the regular season undefeated.

In addition to becoming special-teams coach, I was the team "doctor." Of course, I'm not an actual doctor. None of the inner-city teams had the medical support of physical trainers and doctors so commonly available to suburban teams. I took a Red Cross course and purchased medical supplies at a wholesale medical warehouse in Pontiac, Michigan. The Detroit Public Schools Community District provided an ambulance at the games, as previously mentioned. Ironically, however, most injuries occurred during the five weekly practices, so I was there to do what I could.

I spent the years 2010, 2011, and 2012 with the team. Prior to my time in Detroit, I had never understood what it is like growing up in the inner cities of the United States of America. I know better now what these youths' lives are really like.

My three years spent with these players on almost a daily basis provided an incredible learning experience that remains with me today. My brief exposure to their lives certainly does not provide an all-inclusive treatise on growing up black and male in a large inner city. I do, however, want to share my observations derived from close personal friendships with my players, some of which continue to this day. Hopefully, these stories will give you a new perspective on their perilous climb to manhood.

Deficient Schools

I received a copy of the *Detroit Free Press*, which had just concluded a twelve-month study of the lives of children living in Detroit's inner city. The following statistics were obtained for the period January 1, 2009, to September 9, 2015:

- 58 percent of children age seventeen and under lived in poverty.
- 29 percent of those children age seventeen and under lived in extreme poverty.
- $20,500 was the median income of families with children under the age of eighteen.
- 79 percent of Detroit children were African American.
- 13 percent of Detroit children were white.
- 8 percent of Detroit children were Hispanic or other ethnicities.
- 3 percent of Detroit children were proficient in all academic subjects.
- 77 percent of Detroit children became high school graduates.
- 3 percent of Detroit high school graduates were considered college ready.
- 73 percent of Detroit children lived in a single-parent family.
- 43 percent of Detroit children were victims of violent crimes.

Two of those statistics jump out at me:

- 77 percent of Detroit children became high school graduates.
- 3 percent of Detroit high school graduates were considered college ready.

We are pushing kids through the school system unprepared to compete in an ever-increasingly sophisticated job environment.

I'm sure the above statistics can roughly apply to poverty-stricken areas in all our cities, large and small. If you could avoid it, you wouldn't send your child to an inner-city school.

I can only tell you about the high school I know; it is not representative of all the high schools in Detroit, but certainly most of them. Our school had numerous dedicated teachers and administrative staff who did everything they could to make the learning experience a successful one. We had graduates who went onto college and obtained degrees.

We also had many who dropped out or were expelled along the way. There were too many absent students whose parents did not mandate school attendance. Books were not available to every student. Some classes had the students push two desks together so they could share a book while in class, but they were not permitted to take the book out of the classroom.

Our school had ten security officers stationed throughout the school. Metal detectors were used at the only entrance for incoming students. The counselors were overworked; students often had trouble in school because of the traumas of their family lives.

All too often, obtaining a high school diploma in Detroit doesn't necessarily mean our graduates can move on to college on the same terms as a graduate from a suburban high school. As an example, one of our players graduated with a 2.7 grade point and a 14 ACT score. Most of the students I knew had a 13 or 14 ACT score. He applied to Wayne State University in downtown Detroit. Because of his low ACT score, he had to take what they refer to as "remedial classes," which do not count for college credit. The typical remedial classes required are math and English. He was a full-time student at Wayne State for two years before he was allowed to choose a major.

Some of our players did not have the necessary credits to graduate with a diploma. In these cases, they merely had to sit at a computer, learn the subject matter, and pass the subsequent tests. It was a well-designed and expedient way to make up the missing courses and still graduate on time. Unfortunately, one day after school, while attending the online school, one of the players got into a fight, and another player came to his rescue. They were both expelled and have not obtained their high school diplomas as of four years later. If some of our ex-players do eventually earn a college degree, they will almost certainly become the first males in their families to graduate.

It was always true that inner-city kids could join the military if college wasn't for them. Today, however, the entrance test for all the services is the Armed Services Vocational Aptitude Battery (ASVAB). The average high school graduate from an inner-city high school cannot pass this test. The military requires a higher IQ than ever before, due to the more advanced technology involved in modern weaponry. If, however, an individual is earnest about passing the ASVAB and entering military service, there are study materials, practice tests, and hopefully tutors for those subjects never taught as part of the person's high school curriculum. I have taken some of our players to recruiting offices and seen them fail. So military service is another door of opportunity closed to them unless the person mounts a major effort to fill in his or her knowledge holes.

In addition to a grossly inferior education, the following sections highlight other issues poor kids have that make living a daily exercise in survival.

Accidental Deaths

In my second year as an assistant football coach, a young freshman came out for the team. He was not a natural athlete, but he displayed great effort and a desire to improve his skills. The coaches and players got a kick out of his enthusiasm and sense of humor. He practiced with us during the hot summer months and got to play in four junior varsity games. On a Monday morning in October, we were informed that he had accidentally been shot and killed in the basement of his home. He and a friend were playing with his father's gun, which they didn't think was ready to fire. His friend aimed the gun at him, killing him instantly. Of course, it was a terrible tragedy for his family and friends and all of us who worked with him every day.

When people read about this, they may ask why a loaded gun was in the house in the reach of children. I don't know where the gun was located or how the kids found it. I do know, however, that there are numerous home invasions in the city, and many people have some kind of weapon for self-defense. It's just a fact of life there.

The school rented a bus for any team members who wanted to attend the funeral. All the coaches came that day, as well as about twenty players. It was obvious to my wife and me that this was not the first funeral our players had attended for a young person gone too soon. The team wore his jersey number on their helmets for the remainder of the season.

Hunger

President Dwight Eisenhower, Commanding General of the Normandy invasion in World War II, once said, "Every gun that is made, every warship launched, every rocket fired, signifies in the final sense a theft from those who hunger and are not fed, those who are cold and are not clothed."

One evening at about ten o'clock at night, we received a call from a young man. He explained that there was no food in the house for him, his mother, and his brothers and sisters. He was asking if we could buy some loaves of bread and bologna that could feed his family until the next welfare check arrived in about a week. There happened to be a neighborhood grocery store that was still open at that hour, so we drove to his house and took him to the store. He made good selections, with the help of my wife.

On the way home, he explained that he didn't think his mother made good food-buying decisions that could enable a family his size to have adequate food throughout the month. Her tendency was to buy food that everybody likes but that is not necessarily healthy—which is a common practice in impoverished families. Also, some families may not have all necessary kitchen appliances in working order and available for cooking meals from scratch.

Recurring hunger is a common dilemma in the city. Some families run out of food days before the next welfare check arrives. Another reason for a shortage sometimes can be that the money is spent on lottery tickets and other non-food items.

When high schools are in session, free breakfast and lunches are provided. It is not uncommon that the food provided at school will be students' only food for the day. We had players show up for their four o'clock practice after not having had anything to eat all day. They just didn't want to eat the food being provided by the school that day.

Holidays are also looked upon differently in the city than in the suburbs. Although suburban kids enjoy holiday and summer breaks away from school, inner-city kids don't eat as well when the schools' meals are not there for them. So holidays are an upper for some and a downer for others.

Kids with Lead Poisoning

The Mayo Clinic tells us that lead poisoning occurs when lead builds up in a child's body. Even small amounts of lead can cause serious health problems. Young children are especially vulnerable to lead poisoning, which can severely affect mental and physical development. Lead poisoning can also be fatal. The most common sources of lead poisoning in children are lead-based paint and lead-contaminated dust in older homes.

Many poor families live in very old houses or apartments that have lead-based paint. When old windows are opened and closed, paint fragments and dust can fall to the floor, where a baby is crawling around. All babies like to put things in their mouths that they find along the way. Their water supply may also be conveyed through very old, swollen lead pipes. Little kids contract varying degrees of this lethal menace even before they begin to attend school. Lead poisoning in poverty-stricken areas is a big, serious problem.

In some inner-city schools, 20 to 40 percent of the kids have lead poisoning. They begin attending school in special education classes if their condition is detected early enough, or they are thrown in with the general population, only to discover that they can't keep up. Last year, the Detroit Public Schools Community District was two hundred teachers short of its needs. The biggest teacher shortage in these inner-city schools is always special education teachers.

Inadequate Clothing

One evening after school, Nancy and I dropped by at the school to give some kids a ride home. It was long after the end of football season on a cold February day that registered about five degrees Fahrenheit. The kids were all familiar, except for a newcomer who was with them. Although he was obviously African American, his skin was a reddish purple in color. He was shivering and wearing only a sweatshirt. When asked, he admitted that he didn't own a coat. He still decided, however, that he would tough it out, because he didn't want to miss a day of school.

After we dropped the other kids at their homes, we went in search of a winter coat. He knew exactly where we should go. On a street corner not far from his house was a combination gas station and coat store. The owner was just closing up for the day, but we told him that we were there to buy a coat for this young man. He reopened the store, and the young man went straight, without any hesitation, to the coat he wanted. After we purchased it, he told us that he had been in that store often and loved that coat but knew he would never own it. Well, he walked out of the store wearing that coat. During the short remaining trip to his house, he said no one had ever done something like that for him, especially strangers. There are millions of inner-city kids in the United States who see what suburban kids wear and would like to wear trendy things too. It's not difficult to make a difference in the life of someone who has nothing!

Empty Bleachers

A reality about being a football player in the city is that hardly any family members see their sons, grandsons, or brothers play. One reason is that few adults in the inner-city own a car.

As I mentioned previously, during the same seasons that I was at Henry Ford High, we had two grandsons playing high school football at two different suburban schools. All the parking lots at those games were overflowing with cars, and the attendance varied from eight hundred to fifteen hundred fans.

What a downer for inner-city athletes! All high school football players undergo grueling hours and days in the weight room and on the practice field preparing for those seven games each season. The conditioning begins immediately after the previous season has ended, and on-field practices are conducted during the steaming hot days of summer.

Some players need to take one or two buses to make it to summer practices. City buses don't always run on a predictable schedule, so the player has to leave home one to two hours before practice begins so that he will be able to successfully navigate his way through the city to the practice field in time.

As the season drags on into late September and October, it is dark and cold as practice ends, and these youths make their way to the bus stop for the ride home. It could take another two hours to actually arrive home after waiting at the bus stop for a long time, because there are fewer buses in the evening.

After all of this effort, the big day comes for a game. If it is an away game, there may be no one in the stands on the team's side of the field—except, during my three years, Nancy, who came with me to all the games. Because away games are home games for the other team, there may be between twenty-five and fifty people on their side. On our home games, the reverse was true. The visiting team would have no one, and we would have twenty-five to fifty fans.

When we attended our grandsons' games in suburbia, however, the home team would have about six hundred people, and the visitors would have one to two hundred fans. The really big games saw one to two *thousand* total fans. I truly can't imagine how our players felt about playing before empty stands. Not one player ever mentioned that he wished his family members could have seen him play. It was yet another example of their disappointment merging into quiet acceptance.

Family Members in Prison

A number of our players had family members in prison during the four years they played on the team. They would tell me about their brother, cousin, father, mother or uncle who was serving time. They were in constant states of worry that their incarcerated loved ones would be harmed in prison or change into completely different people once released. Many players lacked the money to visit family members in prisons located a long distance from Detroit, so it was difficult to communicate with and be a source of support to those serving time.

The number of inner-city families who have or have had a loved one behind bars is staggering. Sometimes both parents end up serving time. Because most families are single-parent families in the city, the imprisonment of moms throws tremendous responsibility onto the oldest children. Hopefully a grandmother or aunt can help support a household suddenly being led by a sixteen-year-old.

Many of the football players I knew had a brother or sister gone for years. When they returned home, prison life had changed them, usually for the worse. Many couldn't get jobs with prison records in their pasts. Hopelessness, frustration, and anger sometimes caused them to do things that landed them back in prison for a second or third time.

Drive-By Shootings

From time to time, we read about drive-by shootings in which some innocent adult or child is wounded or killed. Sometimes the shootings are targeted at a certain member of the household, and at other times they are random. One young man was attending a house party a few years before entering high school. While he was enjoying the party, shots rang out from a passing car, sending people running for cover in all directions. As a young boy, he was as scared as everyone else at the party.

When the shooting stopped, he ran for home as fast as he could. He felt no pain while running but discovered, when entering his house, that he was spilling blood out of his shoe. He rolled up his pant leg to find the source and discovered a bullet had gone through the muscle of his right calf and exited without striking a bone. The two scars of entry and exit are still visible today.

I think this episode illustrates the reality that those who spend their lives in the inner-cities of large metropolitan areas are always in danger of being in the wrong place at the wrong time.

Random Assaults

As I related earlier, many of our fall practices ended just as it was getting dark. Only about five players would have a ride waiting to take them home. The others walked or waited for the bus.

One night a player took the bus from the school to another bus stop, where he waited to transfer to a second bus that would take him the rest of the way home. He was alone at the second bus stop when a man approached him suddenly with a gun in his hand. He put the muzzle of the gun against the player's cheekbone. He demanded any money this high school youth had and his cell phone. As the player related to me the next day, he thought his life was over. Fortunately, the man ran off, sparing the player's life.

In another incident, one of our players was walking home from practice when a man came up from behind him and stabbed him in the upper back. Luckily for the player, the knife's blade glanced off his left shoulder blade, breaking the skin but not going deeper. Again, it was a robbery attempt in darkness. The man fled after getting what he wanted. Both players reported to practice the day following the attacks and returned home after practice the way they always had.

Very Few Cars

Transportation in Detroit is another serious problem. Most single-parent families do not have a car. Their means of getting around are either on foot, in a friend's car, or on the city bus. I just priced car insurance for a leased 2007 Chevy Malibu driven by a resident who lives in a zip code near the high school where most of our ex-players live. The monthly insurance payment would be $798.68. This assumes that the driver has good credit and a good driving record. The auto insurance premiums in Detroit are astronomical because so many accidents are caused by uninsured drivers and also because many cars are stolen. Most people in the city cannot afford to lease or buy a car, maintain it, and pay eight hundred dollars per month in auto insurance.

There are numerous used car dealers in the inner city. Those who can afford a car usually buy from one of the used car companies near their homes. Some of the dealers will also rent a car by the month. If, however, you fall behind on your monthly rent, the dealer can locate the car with GPS and remotely shut the car down so that it can't be driven. This makes it easy to reclaim the car, and then the renter is done.

At our high school, which had fourteen hundred students when I was involved, there was only one car in the student parking lot; our team's quarterback owned that car. In the suburban high schools, you'll see four to six hundred student cars on a normal school day.

Another indicator of the transportation problem is that neighborhood grocery stores erect barriers in front of them so that shopping carts cannot be removed from the immediate area next to the building. This is to prohibit shoppers from keeping their groceries in a cart and pushing it all the way home, since these shoppers mostly lack cars. This lack of adequate transportation is also one of the main reasons, as I previously mentioned, why family members are unable to attend school events.

Rampant Disappointment

When most kids discover they aren't going to have something they were looking forward to receiving, they are disappointed. They usually express their disappointment in many ways. These reactions can include anger, verbalization of their disappointment, and even tantrums of various kinds.

The average black male youth growing up in an inner-city usually reacts to disappointment with silence. He has been disappointed so often throughout his young life that he is not surprised when another disappointment crops up. He has developed a defense mechanism called acceptance, which enables him to move on. Unfortunately, this cycle often leads to the demise of hope at an early age.

The most common aspiration I saw young black teens express was that they would manage to stay alive until at least age twenty-one. Many young men they knew or knew of were either dead or in prison by the time they reached twenty-one. I spoke with a twenty-three-year-old inner-city dweller who was proud of the fact that he had made it so far. He began hearing gunshots outside his bedroom window when he was nine years old. The day I spoke with him, he was working in the suburbs and was fearful of returning to the only home he could afford, which was located in a violent area. He told me that he didn't know of anyone who was looking to harm him specifically, but he had seen many people killed by random gunshots not actually intended for the victims.

These youths often mask their many disappointments with laughter and a remarkable sense of humor. Probably the best example of their sense of humor happened one August day in 2011. Our head coach had arranged for a preseason practice game with another school in a nearby state. It was a very exciting occasion for our kids, most of whom had never traveled beyond the Detroit city limits. The school provided a bus for the team, and we rented a second bus for any family members who wanted to come along. We filled the family bus, so many of our boys, for the very first time, would have a loved one actually in attendance at one of their games.

When we took the field, there was a large crowd already filling the bleachers on the home team side. The opposing team came out for their warm-ups and appeared to be completely white players with no players of color. As the game began, the referees from the local area began calling penalties against our team, and they seemed to be questionable calls. The other team was a very good team, and their players began scoring on us.

As the game went along, it became obvious that the referees were being very unfair to our players. It was blatant racial discrimination. At the age of seventy, I had never personally experienced discrimination. I became outraged much more so than our coaches and players. In the middle of the third quarter, I ran out onto the middle of the field, stopping the game and yelling, "This is bullshit!" All four referees ran over to find out why I was so upset. I told them in plain English that they had been racially discriminating against my black players. I said, "You guys don't have to take this game away from our kids. Your team is good enough to beat us without your help. Each of you should be ashamed of yourselves."

When I returned to our bench, the players and coaches appreciated my sticking up for them, but they just wanted to finish the game and head home. I was still upset about the way our kids were treated, but the players, who had experienced so much disappointment in their young lives,

---

had moved on. The ride home was one of laughing and joking with one another. We went undefeated thereafter.

Here are some things we did that could be inspirations for you if you are thinking of helping inner-city kids in your community:

1. Help acquire varsity jackets for the athletes. (These greatly boosted my players' self-esteem.)
2. Help acquire varsity jackets for academic achievement.
3. Help acquire needed athletic equipment for various sports.
4. Provide free pizza and soft drinks for team members after each game.
5. Adopt a room, and fully equip it. (We completely funded a new weight room.)
6. Help fund and staff an after-school program. (Kids need a safe place to go.)
7. Fund a school bus to take family members to away games.
8. Collect food for kids over the holidays when school meals aren't available.

Coping Skills (A Survival Story)

I would like to follow up on the topic of rampant disappointment with the following true story of a young boy who survived an incredible ordeal:

At the age of ten, in 1943, while a little boy was living in his home in Japan, American bombers began bombing the Japanese mainland regularly. Because of the rising death toll of its citizens, the Japanese government issued a decree that young children, too young to join the army, should relocate away from the urban areas being bombed to rural areas in the countryside. So, this boy was sent to live with twenty-five other kids in a Buddhist temple out in the country. A schoolteacher lived with them and taught all subjects.

Because food was scarce and always sent first to soldiers, sailors, and airmen fighting in the War, the kids had little food. They learned to catch, with their bare hands, locusts that were infesting farmers' fields nearby. The farmers were glad to see the kids kill as many locusts as possible. The kids would bring the locusts back to the temple, fry them, and eat them. This provided protein in their diet. They also learned to grow sweet potatoes, which gave them carbohydrates. There were, of course, many days when there was not enough food for all the kids. This young boy, when we met as adults, told me that you have no idea what starvation is like until you experience it for yourself.

A school in his city signed a ten-month contract with the temple to provide a teacher who would travel from the city out to the temple each day to conduct classes. This young boy lived at the temple for ten months, during which time his parents only visited him three times. When the temple's contract was completed, the little boy moved back to the city to live in his house with his parents and his grandmother. He'd left for the country as a ten-year-old little boy and returned as a toughened survivor who'd learned that he did not have to rely on anyone other than himself. While back at home, he decided to bury some food in the backyard in a plastic bag in case it would be needed in an emergency.

A few weeks after he returned home, an American bomb landed near his home, destroying it completely. Luckily, he and his family escaped unharmed. He went to the backyard to retrieve his hidden food supply. He dug it up and for a brief moment was distracted by something. When he turned back to his bag of food, it was gone. As he stated, "I was sad and mad." He was sad that he now had no food and mad that someone would do that to him. The longer he thought about it, however, he realized that the person who stole it was also trying to survive. So he decided that when something bad happens to you, anger is not the solution. Just pick yourself up, and keep moving forward.

After the War, he attended medical school in Japan. The quality of medical schools in Japan had deteriorated, because the young professors who'd taught there before the War had died as pilots, soldiers, and sailors. Those remaining to teach were older professors, who were quite out of touch with the latest medical procedures. One day, he told one of his professors he would like to attend an American medical school upon his graduation in Japan, but it was probably impossible because he had no money. The professor told him that there was a scholarship program that was named after an American United States Senator, J. William Fulbright.

According to the US Bureau of Educational and Cultural Affairs, "the Fulbright-Hays Program—a Fulbright Program funded by a Congressional appropriation to the United States Department of Education—awards grants to individual US pre-teachers, teachers, administrators, pre-doctoral students, and postdoctoral faculty, as well as to US institutions and organizations. Funding supports research and training efforts overseas, which focus on non-Western foreign languages and area studies."

This young man applied for the scholarship and won it. After graduating from medical school in Japan, he traveled to the University of California at Berkeley and completed its graduate program, obtaining a PhD in Biochemistry. He met his future wife there and upon graduation began twenty years of service at the National Institutes of Health (NIH) in Washington, DC, as its senior eye researcher. Subsequently, he became a professor and the director of research at the Wayne State University Medical School. He is now retired. Although he lost friends killed by the American bombings during his childhood, he is grateful to this country for the opportunities he has enjoyed as a US citizen.

This gentleman feels that those ten months in the temple prepared him to face life challenges with a strong belief in himself and in his ability to survive. He also has indicated that children should be challenged by their parents and not given everything. He feels parents should make children work for things, which will help develop children's self-esteem and strong personal character along the way.

The Coping Skills of Inner City Kids

One of the ironies of inner-city living is that most kids, in order to make it through each day, have developed superior coping skills. They live in an environment that does not provide financial security or physical safety. Unlike many suburban kids, they have not been spoiled. On the contrary, their childhoods, in many instances, have been ones of deprivation. Yet they take the hand that's been dealt them and do what they can with it. They, in many cases, have not had much help and don't expect it. If some act of kindness happens to come their way, however, they are exceedingly grateful.

This is the big reward for loving these kids. You know you are making a difference with your life!

Building Walls

An article appeared in the July/August 2016 issue of *The Atlantic Magazine* entitled, "The War on Stupid People." It was written by David H. Freeman, and I think it is relevant to a discussion about the walls we build in our own lives.

He begins by pointing out that high intelligence was not a prerequisite for success in the business world back in the middle of the last century. Employers looked for other personal qualities, including a person's work ethic, integrity, family background, and appearance.

In the 2010s, however, he feels that not having a high IQ is a real liability. Of course, the digital world requires the ability to perform tasks that were not even in existence in the 1950s. The road to helping unintelligent people become intelligent is a difficult one, but studies have shown that it is possible. He suggests two methods that can bring this about: reducing poverty and getting at-risk kids into early education programs. There is a strong relationship between poverty and learning difficulty in school.

He rightfully claims, however, that neither society nor the federal government is willing to make dramatic strides in reducing poverty. The only other option is early education for the kids of poor families. If early education is begun at age three, with qualified teachers, it can lift kids' IQs. Assuming this is followed by a quality education after the preschool years, dramatic, positive results can be the outcome. Some of these results include better grades, higher income, crime avoidance, and enhanced personal health. He concludes with the disappointing fact that most public early education programs rarely obtain these results.

How do you respond to the claims summarized from this article? I agree that poverty and the absence of quality early childhood education programs are negative influences on individuals' ability to develop higher intelligence. I think the writer of the article used the term "stupid people" to draw attention to his article. It is a denigrating term that is, however, unnecessarily hurtful.

To identify members of our society as being of a lower class because of lower scores on an SAT or ACT is a big step in the wrong direction for the health of our society. And why would a potential employer assume that having a higher intelligence guarantees that someone would be a better employee? People with high intellects could behave in an arrogant manner and be less empathetic with an unhappy customer than someone with average intelligence. To my knowledge, there is no link between intelligence and effective decision-making. Common sense is not learned in the classroom.

As this book is being written, there is much discussion about building a wall along the southern border of the United States. Some are in favor, some opposed. Think, however, of all the walls we have built in our lifetime. We build walls of all kinds: religious, racial, ethnic, financial, intellectual, geographical, social, political, and educational. We also build walls between immigrants or native-born citizens. Because of all of these walls, we don't have the interpersonal cohesiveness we need to survive as a society.

Nelson Mandela, the former president of South Africa, once said, "No one is born hating another person because of the color of his skin, or his background, or his religion. People must learn to hate, and if they can learn to hate, they can be taught to love, for love comes more naturally to the human heart than its opposite." The larger issue, however, is that we've got to stop labeling fellow Americans if we are going to have a kinder, gentler, and more loving society. We have to break down all of these walls we've created and see one another as fellow citizens deserving of our love and respect. As Abraham Lincoln once said, "America will never be destroyed from the outside. If we falter and lose our freedoms, it will be because we destroyed ourselves."

In order to create a more sustainable society, we'll actually have to consider doing something that we have perhaps not thought of doing ever before in our lives: We'll have to *decide* to love strangers who may or may not love us in return.

What Are Your Motives?

A friend of mine who was a senior officer of a local bank volunteered each Tuesday during his lunch hour to help distribute food to needy families in Detroit. He called us one day to say that he'd met a family with a very young mother who was in desperate need of clothing for her six children and herself. We had six young children at the time, and our kids' clothes would match up well with her family. When we met her, we discovered that she was living in an abandoned house.

We brought her food and clothing and soon realized she would be evicted, with nowhere to live. We bought a small, very modest house for eight thousand dollars that served as her family home for about eight years. Her children were rough on the house, and it was obvious that they were growing up and needed a larger house. We sold the small house and bought a larger brick home with a second floor and a basement for twenty-one thousand dollars. I told her that if she took good care of this house and I could sell it eventually at a profit, she would receive half of the profit to use if she decided to move elsewhere.

Her family lived in this house for about five years. By this time, her older children wanted to live on their own, and she decided to move back to her hometown in the South. I was only able to sell this house for seventeen thousand dollars, thereby incurring a four-thousand-dollar loss. Because I had a mortgage on the property, I had to come up with the four thousand dollars in order to give the purchaser clear title. When I explained to her that I didn't have a profit to share with her, she didn't understand and became angry with me. Because she had no formal education and had faced many disappointments, she felt I had deceived her, and our thirteen-year friendship ended on a sour note. After all we had done for her family over all of those years, her response was upsetting to us.

We didn't regret all our efforts on her behalf, however, because we knew that helping her was the right thing to do. We didn't hear from her again for the next five years. One day, our phone rang, and it was her calling. I wasn't at home at the time, and Nancy took the call. She explained that her life was much better now and that she had a good job back in her hometown working at a local nursing home. She was also happy to report that all six of her children were still alive. She said that the purpose of her call was to thank us for the support we had given her all of those years while she was trying to raise her children alone in Detroit. We didn't do what we did in order to receive some form of gratitude, but it gave us a better ending to the story.

As Maya Angelou, the prominent African American poet, once said, "Try to be a rainbow in someone's cloud. Many people live under a cloud. If we are going to prevent the unraveling of our present day society, someone else's cloud must become our concern as well as theirs."

Single Parents

Are Single Parents Forgotten Flowers?

The heroes in our society, in my opinion, are single parents, who are in most cases single moms. Children growing up in single-parent families typically do not have the same economic or human resources available as those growing up in two-parent families. Compared with children in married-couple families, children raised in single-parent households are more likely to drop out of school, to have or cause a teen pregnancy and to experience a divorce in adulthood.[1]

The US Census Bureau also reports that between 1960 and 2013, the proportion of black children living in a single-parent home more than doubled, from 22 percent to 55 percent. For white children, the percentage tripled, from 7 percent to 22 percent.

---

[1] datacenter.kidscount.org. Page title, "Children in single parent families"

Single parents must face the challenges of earning a living and raising children too often without the daily support of the one with whom they probably once shared a common vision of life. As difficult as this situation is for the single parent, it can also have a lifelong detrimental impact on the parent's child or children. Regardless of the reasons that caused this situation, the primary focus must be on the wellbeing of the children, who are innocent.

There is usually and understandably a difficult and emotionally charged history between the mother and father when the mother is not a single mother by choice. Constant recrimination between the two parents and other destructive behavior can materially destroy their children's self-esteem. This is especially true if the children feel they are the cause of the breakup. In adulthood, these children often struggle when attempting to build lasting relationships with future partners.

I know that we all want to get through this life with as few regrets as possible. In later years, it would be comforting to look back and know that every effort was made to help the children of a single parent enter adulthood with confidence and a healthy sense of self-esteem.

Will you become a source of comfort and support to a single parent?

The Elderly

Are the Elderly Forgotten Flowers?

In the United States, we have a large aging population. Many elderly people reside in assisted-living centers or in their homes alone. They are often lonely and, in many cases, the forgotten generation.

I remember when my ninety-three-year-old grandmother was living in a senior citizen facility in downtown Detroit. She was my mother's mom. She had lived a tough life and had migrated from Ireland after only having received a third-grade education. She was pulled out of school and sent to care for a dying relative. She had two sisters, one of whom died of seasickness while the three of them were making the journey back to the United States after visiting their father when they were young adults. I visited her often with my mom and still remember all the older people sitting together in a room with chairs along each wall. Each of the chairs was occupied by a person looking straight ahead and wondering when it would be his or her time to meet his or her maker. My dad was great at accompanying my mom on her frequent visits. When they entered her room, my grandmother would say, "Paula, who is this man you brought with you?" Obviously, she had forgotten who my dad was, but she always recognized her daughter.

Nancy had a grandmother, Mimi, who was living in the same senior center after her husband, Baba, died. Nancy made frequent visits to her grandmother to help compensate for the lonely hours. She and Mimi were very close because Nancy was her only granddaughter. From her earliest days, Nancy spent many days and nights at Mimi and Baba's modest home on Detroit's eastside.

One day, after we had been married for about eight years, Nancy was playing tennis at our local tennis club in the Detroit suburbs. In the middle of a game, she suddenly had an overwhelming feeling that she should go to visit Mimi. She stopped playing and told her tennis opponent she had to go. She ran to her car without changing out of her tennis clothes and drove the John Lodge Expressway straight downtown to Detroit to visit Mimi. When she entered the senior center, the doorman told her she was not dressed appropriately and could not enter the building. When he turned to speak with someone else, she made a mad dash for the elevator door that was open. She walked into Mimi's room and over to her bed. She took Mimi's hand in hers and said, "It won't be long now, and you'll be with Baba." In a few moments, without saying a word, Mimi died. Sometimes, dying people will hang on until they can see a loved one once again. Nancy will always be grateful that she was there with her at the end.

Nancy also had a great aunt, Theresa, who was widowed and living in a senior center on the east side of Detroit, in Macomb County. Nancy would take our toddler grandson to visit Theresa and share lunch with her. He was the source of smiles from many of the patients and staff members.

In 1939, Theresa and her husband Steve were living in Austria at the beginning of World War II. They were farmers. When the Nazis annexed Austria, they took her husband and many other Austrian men away to work for the German Army. He was gone from 1939 until the end of the war in 1945. All of that time, she never heard from him and presumed he was dead.

Some months after the end of the war, she was out working in the fields on their farm and noticed a man walking toward her in the far distance. As he came closer, she could see that it was Steve. He had walked home from World War II. The terrible things he'd seen in those missing six years were always locked up in his memory. Steve and Theresa made it to the United States and lived a good life in a Detroit suburb.

Every one of these older people has a story to tell. They also have wisdom and valuable life lessons to share with those willing to listen. All they need is someone who cares enough to take an interest in them. Your visit is a gift to them.

Make the world a better place for a senior in your family or at a local senior center!

Veterans

Are Local Veterans Forgotten Flowers?

Veteran hospitals are filled with the people who fought our wars and paid a dear price for their loyalty and courage.

Many of them will remain in the hospital until their injuries are healed. Others, however, will never leave because of the severity of their wounds.

For a time, shortly after we were married, Nancy volunteered as a chaplain's assistant at the huge Veterans Affairs hospital in Allen Park, a suburb of Detroit. She was saddened to see so many lonely people, some of whom had wounds that would not permit them to speak. The fourth floor was the home of those men who had tracheotomies performed on them. Nancy took a special interest in them in an attempt to make her time with them more comforting than all the hours, months, and years they endured without visitors. One man in particular, Steve, and she would communicate with written notes passed between them.

On one of her visits to the hospital, she happened to meet an older woman who had been a senior officer in the army during World War II. She was one of only three female patients in the hospital. They struck up a friendship, and Nancy learned that the lady had served on General Eisenhower's personal staff during the Normandy Invasion in France on June 6, 1944. She needed a wheelchair when Nancy met her, and she had not been out of the hospital very often in all the years she'd spent there.

Nancy arranged to take her, wheelchair and all, down to the Renaissance Center in downtown Detroit, located right on the beautiful Detroit River. It is an international waterway and part of the St. Lawrence Seaway, which hosts cargo ships from all over the world. The "Ren Cen" is very modern, with a circular design and large windows. The elevator faces the water, and her guest really loved the spectacular sights on the elevator trip to the top floor where the restaurant was located. Her day spent on this outing gave her great joy. On a subsequent visit to the hospital, Nancy was told by the chaplain that her newfound friend had passed away.

Of course, today the Veterans Affairs hospitals are filled with veterans of our most recent wars in Iraq and Afghanistan. The population is much younger than those veterans Nancy met almost fifty years ago. Many vets were called back to these wars as many as four and five times because of a shortage of personnel with their particular expertise. These younger vets, however, have all the same issues of their predecessors: loneliness, physical wounds, and post-traumatic stress disorder.

Consider dropping by a veteran's hospital to "be a rainbow in someone's cloud." Go to the chaplain's office, and ask him or her to direct you to a patient or patients who could greatly benefit from your visit. It is always gratifying to do the right thing for someone else. As the saying goes, "It is in giving that we receive."

They showed the courage to fulfill their obligation to us. Have the courage to personally thank them for their service.

3

~∞~   ~∞~

Is There a Forgotten Flower You Will Help?

You have seen many examples of forgotten flowers. Is there a forgotten flower or flowers you are going to help? Do you want to make a positive difference in the life of someone you know or may not know?

People You Know

Love begins by taking care of the closest ones—the ones at home.

—Mother Teresa

Are you a forgotten flower? How about your spouse, children, parents, siblings, or friends? If you think about them one at a time, you will probably be able to identify someone who may feel left behind. Your first responsibility is to reach out with a helping hand to people you know.

People You Don't Know

How wonderful it is that nobody need wait a single moment before starting to improve the world.

—Anne Frank

Most of us don't take an interest in those who live in our communities beyond our family members and friends. You wouldn't, however, have to travel far in order to find people living desperate lives with little or no hope for their futures or those of their children. This is the great dilemma of our present-day society. Most people are so busy that they don't see the needs of people they don't know.

Hundreds or even thousands of children in your metro area go to bed hungry. All too many of them are receiving a substandard education that will guarantee their failure as adults. When today's deprived children have children of their own, the cycle of despair and hopelessness will repeat itself with predictable results.

As Elie Wiesel, a writer and Holocaust survivor, famously wrote, "The opposite of love is not hate. It's indifference."

Are we indifferent to the hopeless lives of those who live in our midst? If yes, will we always be indifferent to them? Can you—will you—take an interest in the plight of those living in poverty in your own community?

If not you, who? If not now, when?

How Can You Love the Forgotten Flowers?

It's not too late to make a positive difference with your life! There are many things you can do. I think they fall into four categories: time, talent, treasure, and influence.

Time

For some people, daily responsibilities don't allow for much free time to reach out to others. Our lives are always reduced to a matter of priorities. Will you take the time to reach out to someone left behind?

Mother Teresa told us, "Bloom where you're planted." Do what you can where you are. She said that there are people in your own neighborhood deserving of your help. Sometimes just a smile or a kind word can brighten a day.

If you have some time, mentoring a child through Big Brothers, Big Sisters offers you a possibility to make a positive difference one child at a time. You could become a tutor to a child who would otherwise never become literate without your help. Remember, every child can be taught. Every child can be saved!

Talent

Do you have a certain talent that could be put to good use for the benefit of someone in need? Most inner-city schools don't have the budget necessary to fully staff all the positions needed to give kids a complete learning experience.

You could volunteer to be a tutor. Many inner-city students will graduate from high school with third and fourth grade reading and writing skills.

You could also help out with a school's athletic programs, as I did.

Many inner-city kids don't have regular medical or dental checkups. If an inner-city high school has a nurse available, he or she is usually only at the school on a part-time basis. Are you able to provide health support?

Inner-city schools also don't have a budget for many extracurricular activities that should be a necessary part of the learning experience. Many have libraries but no full-time librarian. Musical instruments gather dust without a music director. Swimming pools are empty and abandoned without a swimming coach, and on it goes.

Treasure

Do you have financial resources you could use to make a positive difference? Do you know any single parents who are struggling to raise their children and on the ragged edge financially? Also, many local charitable organizations are underfunded and unable to adequately accomplish their mission.

You—alone or with some of your friends—could adopt a school or a department in a school, such as the library, in an impoverished area of your community. These schools usually have extremely limited financial resources, which means that their students will be deprived of many things that are common in more privileged schools. If you investigate one of these financially strapped schools, you'll be shocked to see the circumstances teachers and students must endure.

Influence

Do you belong to an organization that could help? Do you know someone who can devote time and/or treasure to those in need? Do you own a successful business, or are you a senior officer in a successful business that could reach out?

Your Decision

You have been exposed to many ideas intended to help you experience love for people you know and love for people you don't know. What will you do?

It's never too late to make a positive difference with your life!

Printed in the United States
By Bookmasters